STO √

A

G

About the Book Small farms are becoming a thing of the past. No longer is the countryside dotted with red barns so familiar and alive with the noise and activity of animals. Luckily there are some small farms left. One of them is in Dublin, New Hampshire. The Gemmings spent many months there, photographing an unusually varied collection of farm animals. In these engaging and sensitive pictures we see geese, pigs, sheep, donkeys, and many other domesticated animals playing with their young, learning, and just being themselves.

With a narrative perfectly keyed to the photographs, the Gemmings conduct a delightful tour of the barnyard. They explain in clear terms the birth, growth, care, and feeding of these farm creatures. A chart at the end provides a concise reference to important facts about each.

Elizabeth and Klaus Gemming have put together a warm, appealing, and informative book that young readers will enjoy turning to time and again.

ELIZABETH & KLAUS GEMMING

Born in a Barn

Farm Animals and Their Young

COWARD, McCANN & GEOGHEGAN, INC. NEW YORK

SBN: GB-698-30545-0
SBN: TR-698-20293-7

Library of Congress Catalog Card Number: 73-94106
Printed in the United States of America

06209

To Mary Alice and Allan Fox,
Bruce, Ken, and Andy

LONG, LONG AGO the earth's people wandered from place to place. They hunted animals for food. They stole birds' eggs from nests and gathered nuts and fruits where they found them. When food ran out, the people moved on. From time to time, bands of men, women, and children discovered spots where countless animals fed in grassy meadows or wild grain fields, among berry bushes or grapevines. The people settled in these bountiful places.

One day someone noticed that new plants had come up from last year's discarded seeds. Someone else caught a wild goat and her newborn kid, drank some of her milk, and found that it tasted good.

Why not keep the goat and milk her every day? Why not catch and raise a few wild pigs? Why not save seeds for planting? Early farmers learned to keep their animals tied up or fenced in and took good care of them. In return, the animals gave them meat, milk, leather, and wool. Early man soon found out, too, that he could teach young horses or ponies to carry his belongings for him—and even himself and his family.

Gradually the once-wild animals that made their homes with man began to change. The farm, or domestic, animals of today are heavier, slower, weaker, and more peaceful in their ways than their wild cousins—if they were turned loose in the wilderness, many would not be able to take care of themselves.

Not long ago many Americans still lived on small family farms, with a horse to pull the plow, a cow or a milk goat, a pig, a few sheep, and some chickens. This farm is like an old-fashioned family farm. Here comes the rooster now! "Cock-a-doodle-do!" he crows. He seems to say, "Welcome to my farm!"

THE MOTHER HEN is one of the busiest and most devoted mothers on the farm, but the rooster takes no part at all in bringing up chicks. Proud and handsome, he spends most of his time strutting up and down on his strong toes and showing off his glossy feathers and the bright-red comb on the top of his head.

Chickens work out a special system for getting along together. It is called a pecking order, and each chicken knows its exact place. Hens accept roosters as the rulers of the flock, and the roosters fight one another for first place. Hens fight among themselves to set up their own order, squawking and pecking until, one by one, the weaker hens give in and one hen is the winner over all. She is allowed to peck all the other hens, but they can't peck her back. The hen that ranks second can peck all but the first, and so on down the line. The lowest-ranking hens, scrawny and ruffled, cling to the edges of the group. Once this order is established, the whole flock obeys.

Every mother hen recognizes her own chicks. She takes them out on walks around the yard and shows them over and over again how she uses her three-toed feet to scratch for food. The chicks usually learn very fast, by watching and imitating her.

As the little family tours the barnyard, the hen "talks" to her chicks constantly. She makes clucking noises that seem to say, "Follow me!" She calls her chicks to her side with short, low noises. When she finds some grain, she utters a quick "Kuk-kuk-kuk-kuk" and the chicks run to her. She warns them of danger—of hawks or vicious dogs —with long, sharp, high notes. She tries to shield them from turkeys, who can be mean and ill-tempered. Male turkeys make a frightening "gobble-gobble" deep in their throats and often nip at the chicks.

Often during the day and evening the mother hen makes a series of low purring sounds, to coax the chicks to gather in close to her for a rest. The chicks back in under her body, and soon only a few tiny yellow beaks peek out from among her blanketing feathers.

Chickens, like all birds, do not give birth to living babies. They lay eggs. If a rooster and a hen have mated, the egg the hen lays may contain a tiny dark speck that will grow into a chick. The egg must be kept warm—by the hen in her nest or in a heated incubator. The unborn chick will float in a sac of liquid and be nourished by the yolk.

10

In large incubators, eggs are set in trays under heat lamps. Here is a small incubator, a "glass hen" heated by an electric coil and a light bulb to about 100°–103°. A thermometer measures the temperature and the light bulb switches on and off automatically to maintain a constant heat. The transparent cover should not be taken off for more than a few moments or the heat will be lost.

After twenty-one days, an egg is ready to hatch. The chick has used all its food, and it feels cramped in its too-small house. It pecks at the shell and tears the lining, and cracks appear in the shell. The chick pokes its beak through a hole, peeping weakly, then stops to rest, then pecks some more, for hours. At last, the shell breaks open! The newborn chick looks wet, scrawny, and matted. As it sprawls out, exhausted, other chicks clamber over it. It seems to sleep, but then it moves its legs and stubby wings and begins to dry. In two hours it will be just as fluffy as the others.

Incubator chicks can be placed under a hen when they are very young and she will adopt them and train them as her own. Chicks can get along without a mother, though, if they are warm and learn how to eat and drink. After one day in the incubator they are moved to this large open box lined with wood chips. A brooder, or heat lamp, hangs above them, to keep the temperature about 90°. Older chicks peck and eat mash and drink water from a dish, and the littlest chicks quickly learn to copy. Chicks use their eyes to find food—all birds have sharp eyes. Chicks stay under the brooder for six to eight weeks, until they grow their first set of feathers.

Grown-up hens live in the hen house. (Farmers try to make sure all their roosting places are exactly alike, because hens get very jealous.) An average hen lays 250 eggs a year. Hens are supposed to lay eggs in their nests, but now and then they will go into the barn and

lay eggs among the bales of hay. Hens are quarrelsome by nature, but sometimes they squabble and squawk on purpose to confuse and scare away their enemies—the hawks or owls that circle around looking for lost chicks or the raccoons, skunks, or foxes that invade the hen house at night to steal eggs or kill one of the chickens.

On the right is a full-grown domestic turkey gobbler. His over-lapping feathers are deep brown, drabber than the coppery or green-ish-bronze feathers of his wild cousins. Wild turkeys like to roost in trees for the night, but farm turkeys are too heavy to fly. The turkey is a native North American bird. Indians in Mexico were raising tur-

keys at least 400 years ago. The Pilgrims and later settlers hunted wild turkeys for food. Just one hundred years ago our woodlands were still full of wild turkeys, but as farmers cleared the forests the flocks all but disappeared. (Today, little by little, wild turkeys are beginning to be seen again in remote, rugged areas of the Northeast.)

A turkey's beak is short and curved, for picking up seeds and insects. Turkeys love acorns. A pointed knob of skin swells and swings down over the beak when the turkey is excited. Its head is covered with bumpy, waxy, bluish-white skin. This skin turns bright red when the turkey is upset or angry and fades as he calms down. Like other birds, turkeys have earholes but no ear flaps.

GEESE are water birds. They have webbed feet for paddling and thick layers of fat under their skin that allow them to spend hours in the water without getting chilled. Their smoothly layered, oily feathers are water-repellent and so thick that water cannot soak through. They use their long, flexible necks to explore the shallows of ponds and collect weeds and marsh grasses to eat. They let the water strain out of the sides of their broad, flat bills. Their bills are like spoons and are covered with sensitive, leathery skin. Farm geese are cheap to raise because they will also feed on ordinary grass in the barnyard.

Farm geese cannot fly. They look very much like their swimming relatives the swans. The knobs on their bills are for decoration. Like swans, geese can be irritable. They run at intruders with their necks stretched forward, hissing and nipping. These are Brown China geese, with creamy white feathers, tan and brown markings, and black bills. In some countries geese are raised for meat and eggs, but they are most prized for their feathers and the fluffy down of their breasts and underbodies, which are used to stuff pillows and quilts.

Geese are very intelligent and they are unusual among birds and mammals because they mate for life, pairing off and living as families. When a female makes her nest, she lines it with her own down. As she sits on her eggs, the male, or gander, may stand loyally beside her and guard her until they hatch—for a whole month.

A mother goose, like a hen, shows her babies around the yard. She takes her goslings swimming in a big rain puddle. These gray goslings were hatched in an incubator a few days ago, but they have already been adopted. When they were first brought outdoors and set down in the grass, four female geese fought over them, hissing and biting one another. Now one proud goose is their "mother," although for a day or two the others may still try to kidnap them.

COWS look gentle and patient as they gaze at us with their huge, beautiful brown eyes. These cows are Guernseys, known by their fawn-colored coats with white blotches. They have long heads, straight noses, and white foreheads. They live in an old-fashioned cow barn built of weathered timbers, with square windows to let the sunlight in, and dark corners criss-crossed by cobwebs. The barn is small and cozy and smells of the summer hay that gives the cows' milk a fresh, delicious flavor. Each cow has her own stall, with clean straw on

the floor for her bed and a drinking fountain of her own next to her. The cows share the barn with a swift-flying barn swallow that has built her nest of mud and straw on a beam just inside the door. The swallow darts in and out all day with insect food for her babies, huddled deep down in the nest.

Cattle are vegetarians. In summer they eat pasture grass and hay, and in winter they are fed silage, a stored mixture of clover, corn, oats, and alfalfa. A cow scoops up food with her lower jaw. She has thirty-two teeth: twelve grinding molars on top and bottom, and eight incisors, or cutting teeth, on the bottom only. She has no front teeth on top. When she crops grass, she clamps it between her lower teeth and her hard upper gum.

As a cow browses, she swallows her food without chewing it. It goes to a special storage "stomach." Later she looks around for a safe, quiet place where she can settle down to rest. Then, relaxed and drowsy, she brings up the food in small balls called cuds and chews each cud to a pulp, one by one. After that she really swallows the food, which passes through three more stomachs to be completely digested.

Dairy cows are thin and their bones stick out. Their ribs make large barrel-shaped spaces for storing food. Their hind legs are straight and far apart, leaving plenty of room for a large udder, or milk bag. Much of the solid food cows eat is converted into milk, and cows must drink about eight gallons of water a day as well.

Cows are milked twice a day, usually early in the morning and late in the afternoon. Like any female mammal, a cow does not give any milk until she has given birth to a baby. If a cow is to have a calf every year, she is milked for ten months and then given a two-month rest before her new calf is due to be born. Not many farmers milk by hand anymore. This cow is being milked by a milking machine that has four suction attachments to fit on each of her four nipples, or teats. Most cows stand quietly in their stalls to be milked. They like it, because a too-full udder feels very uncomfortable.

A good dairy cow gives about six gallons of milk a day—twenty-four quarts, enough to fill ninety-six glasses. Guernsey milk is yellowish because it contains a large amount of butterfat. The milk can be separated into butterfat (cream) and skim milk. Whole milk sold in stores is usually "homogenized"—treated so it won't separate.

Cows live together in herds without males. Bulls join them only at mating time. Since dairy cows are kept to provide fresh milk for

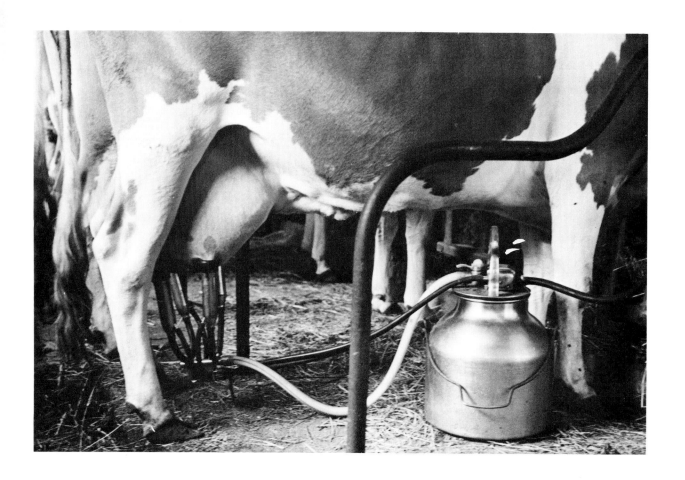

people, their newborn calves are taken from them a few hours after birth. A calf is born wet, but its mother licks it clean and dry. Its legs are very wobbly, but it tries to stand up fifteen minutes after it is born. After it has been taken from its mother, it is taught to drink from a pail with a long rubber nipple—just the way human babies can be fed cows' milk from bottles. An average calf gets two quarts of powdered milk and water formula twice a day. Once it learns how to graze and eat hay, after about five to eight weeks, it does not need milk anymore.

THIS BABY GOAT, or kid, is only fifteen hours old. Its mother is still licking it clean and smoothing its fur with her tongue, but it can already stand and walk without wobbling. It even tries to go down the porch steps! Goats are fast and surefooted, and kids especially love to run and jump and climb on rocks, the steeper the better.

Mother goats usually have twins, but single babies or triplets are fairly common. The mother goat on the page before has, of all things, a beard—many female goats do, and many males do not. It all depends on the breed. It is the same with horns—some goats have them and some don't. (If a kid is going to grow horns, tiny "buds" can be felt on its head soon after birth and begin to show in ten days. These buds are often removed because adult goats can hurt one another badly with their horns. The buds are burned off quickly and it stings for only a minute.)

Goats were probably raised by man as long as 7,000 years ago in Persia. Most farm goats in America are breeds from Switzerland. The mother goat on page 22, who is light tan with white stripes, is a Toggenburg goat originally from the Swiss Alps. Her kid doesn't look

like her at all and probably takes after its father or one of its grand-parents. Goats can be tan, brown, black, white, gray, or a mixture of two or three colors. These tiny, almost-black twin kids and their mother belong to a special small breed called pygmy goats. The white mother and her kid are Angora goats, a breed raised for its long, silky hair.

Generally, farm goats are raised for milking. Milk is a baby's first food, but unfortunately some human babies are allergic to cow's milk. If they are not fed by their own mothers, goats' milk is ideal for them. It is easily digested and rich in minerals. It is whiter and tastes sweeter than cow's milk. A good milk goat gives three or four quarts a day. She gives milk as long as she is milked regularly, but like cows, she is usually allowed to "dry up" and rest before the birth of a new kid.

Her own kids need mother's milk for only two months but will nurse six to eight months if they can.

Like their relatives, cattle and sheep, goats are vegetarians and cud chewers. They especially enjoy hay, alfalfa, oats, corn, apples, and soft tree bark, but they will gladly eat any green plant, with or without flowers on it. Goats have cutting teeth on the bottom jaw only. Kids' teeth are tiny and very sharp. Goats are not at all shy, and they love to chew on shirttails, belt straps, and straw tote bags, and untie shoelaces with their teeth. If you hear that goats eat old tin cans, though, don't believe it. It just isn't true. They do pull paper labels off cans, however, because they like the taste of the glue.

Goats are extremely lively and curious. They are so venturesome, in fact, that their mothers seldom have to nudge them out into the world—they seem to spend more time trying to call them back when they run too far away. Here a mother goat is showing her kid how to drink water from a metal washtub out in the middle of the pasture. While one twin insists on nursing, she keeps pushing the other toward the tub with her nose. The kid is so inquisitive and smart that it quickly learns how to drink.

SHEEP are very closely related to goats, but they are much more placid. They seem quite content to stick together in a flock, and they are easily frightened. This lamb, like all lambs, is very timid. (The tag on its ear is for identification.) Lambs nurse often, for at least two months. They cling to their mothers, bleating in terror if they get lost. In fact, even when a female sheep, or ewe, is grown up, she tends to follow her own mother around. The oldest female in a flock usually becomes the leader.

Most breeds of sheep mate once a year, in the fall, and one or two lambs are born to each mother in the spring, five months less five days after mating. Certain breeds will mate in the spring as well, and their autumn lambs are raised indoors through the winter.

Sheep were among the earliest animals to be raised, by Stone Age tribes of western Asia more than 8,000 years ago. They are very good grazers and eat a lot. They can find food on poor land or in pastures where other animals have already grazed, because they crop grass almost to the roots. They have no upper front teeth, like cattle and goats, and not very many sheep have horns. Sheep are friendly and almost never kick or bite. They love fresh air and sunshine and like to be outdoors on nice days even in winter.

Because of their heavy wool, sheep look fatter than they really are. This ewe has been shorn of her wool and looks rather thin. She is a Dorset, an English breed. Dorsets have woolly heads, broad shoulders, and short, sturdy legs. A good Dorset fleece weighs five to six pounds. The skin under their thick wool is pink. Sheep are shorn once a year, in May or June, when the weather should be mild enough

for them to get used to being without their warm coats. (If the weather turns cool, they have to stay in the barn a day or two so they won't catch cold.)

This old curly-horned ram (who lives by himself in the lower pasture) has been brought up to the porch to be shorn. He has been limping from a sore foot, so the sheepshearer first trims a broken edge on the ram's hoof and takes out a pebble that was stuck between the two "toenails." Then the shearer begins to remove the ram's fleece all in one piece with electric clippers. He shaves off the fleece carefully to avoid nicking the ram's knobby knees. The wool is encrusted with mud and matted with twigs and burs, so it will be cleaned and combed thoroughly before it is spun into yarn for caps, socks, scarves, and mittens.

An active, hardy wild mountain sheep has a double coat: a hairy outer coat, which sheds rain and snow, and a soft undercoat. A domestic sheep has only the undercoat. Here on the left is the long, coarse hair of a Karakul, a wild sheep of western Asia. On the right is the thick, curly wool of a Dorset.

PIGS have heavy bodies, short legs, and thickset heads, and they seem to live to eat—and sleep. (Piglets often sleep head to foot and foot to head in rows.) Pigs are not naturally dirty or lazy, though. There is a good reason why they love to lie down in cool, dark places. They are terribly uncomfortable in warm weather because they have no sweat glands in their skin. They cannot cool off by perspiring, as we can. Pigs get sunburned, too, because they do not have hairy or furry coats to protect their skin. They love to bathe, and if there is no clean water in the barnyard (and there usually isn't), they will happily settle for a mud puddle in the shade. They lie in mud because it feels wet and cool.

A sow usually has eight to ten piglets in a litter. Just before she gives birth, or farrows, she builds a simple nest in the straw of her pen by walking round and round in a circle. Then she settles down inside the circular path she has made. As soon as her piglets are born they begin to root hungrily through the straw with their snouts, following the pathway alongside their mother's belly until each finds a nipple and begins to nurse. The sow just lies there and does nothing else to help her newborns—although she will always guard them fiercely in the face of danger.

Compared to other animal mothers, a sow is selfish. She lets her piglets take care of themselves and does not bother to lick them clean

or nudge them to their feet. She may let them nurse awhile, grunting and wheezing as she lies in the straw, and then just get up and walk away suddenly if she feels like it. Sometimes she rolls over on her stomach and ignores the frantic squeals of her hungry piglets. When they are older and feed on mash from a pan, she often pushes them away and eats all she wants first.

A newborn piglet has a little

short, soft hair. It feels like velvet. The piglet above, ten days old, is just beginning to grow bristles. Piglets are born with sharp little teeth—so sharp, in fact, that once in a while their teeth have to be filed before their mother will let them nurse! When piglets can do without mother's milk, at six weeks, they are called shoats.

Pigs use their round, flat

snouts to root for food. They will eat just about anything: grain mash, vegetables, milk, worms, even assorted garbage, in which they can always find something that tastes good to them. They are not cud chewers like cattle, goats, and sheep, but they do have the same two-part split hoof, made up of two enlarged "toenails" that rest on the ground, with shorter toes behind and above. Pigs could move much faster if only their legs were longer. Piglets do trot surprisingly fast, and they love to

chase one another around the barnyard. They seem to think it is a great game to escape from their pen, but they are quite shy and enjoy running most when there are few people nearby.

Pigs reared for market are called hogs by the age of about seven months, when they should weigh about 240 pounds. Hogs are fattened on special feed made from corn. People have raised pigs for thousands of years, and sausages have been made all over the world since ancient times. Sausages were probably invented in old China, and the Greeks and Romans liked pork sausages too.

The hides of many animals can be treated to make leather, and

pigskin has long been a favorite for gloves. Pigs supply man with bristles for brushes, although many brushes are now made with nylon bristles instead of natural ones.

Hogs are raised to be so fat that many people think all pigs are clumsy, slow, and stupid. Actually, pigs are not dumb—they are more intelligent than cattle and horses. Pigs can be taught to do simple jobs, such as pushing buttons with their snouts to pour food or water into a dish, and usually catch on faster than dogs being taught the same task. Pigs are as clever as any other animal on the farm and make lively playmates.

BABY HORSES, or foals, get to their feet ten to fifteen minutes after they are born. This foal is three days old, and the one on page 41 is ten days old. The foals must nurse until they are about three months old. After that they can live on pasture grass and hay (though they will nurse up to a year). At first foals' legs are so long that they have to bend their knees to be able to reach the grass with their mouths. Horses are vegetarians but not cud chewers. They have full sets of teeth, top and bottom.

Horses were domesticated about 4,500 years ago by wandering tribes in central Asia and used in the hunt and in war. The huge, slow horses that carried knights in armor into battle during the Middle Ages were the ancestors of modern workhorses.

Like cattle, sheep, goats, and pigs, horses are hoofed animals, but horses are different from the others. Instead of a split hoof, they have a hoof that consists of only one "toe." Hooves are natural shoes that enable animals to run great distances over long periods of time without hurting their feet.

A newborn foal has a soft, narrow hoof with a jellylike pad on the bottom that keeps the foot from tearing the sac that surrounds the foal before it is born. A few days after birth the protective pad falls off and a horny sole begins to form. The tough outside of a horse's foot is called the wall. It starts to grow down and forward like a giant toenail to encircle the foot.

Wild horses that run on hard, dry ground wear down the new growth on their hooves automatically. Horses that are kept for occasional riding in the countryside need their hooves filed regularly. Workhorses that pull wagonloads would wear down the walls of their

38

feet very fast, however, if they were not fitted with shoes to keep them from going lame. Racehorses also need shoes to keep their feet from getting sore. Horseshoes are heated red-hot over a charcoal fire and hammered into shape on an iron anvil. After they are shaped, they are cooled and then nailed to the horny wall of the hoof.

Stabled horses may not need shoes, but all horses need their feet cared for regularly. Their feet must be picked clean of dirt and mud and pebbles, and the walls, like toenails, have to be trimmed. (The wall grows at least one-quarter inch a month.) The edges are then neatly filed smooth. A foal's hooves can be trimmed with a sharp knife from the age of three months—and it doesn't hurt a bit.

The young man in the picture is a horseshoer, or farrier. First he uses special tools to clean the grooves of the feet, and then he trims and files the wall. He never cuts the sole or the V-shaped bars that cushion a horse's feet as it runs. He wears a leather apron to protect his legs, and he talks to the horses while he works—horses are often nervous and try to kick or tug their legs away.

DONKEYS are long-eared relatives of horses. They are so closely related to horses that they can be bred with them—the foal of a mare, or female horse, and a male donkey is called a mule. A male donkey is called a jack and a female is called a jennet or jenny. As they graze in the pasture, donkeys look quiet and peaceful, but by nature they are very stubborn, and they bite and kick when they are angry.

The odd egg-shaped bird grazing with the donkeys is a guinea fowl. It is a relative of the pheasant, native to Africa but not commonly raised in America. Long ago, when guinea fowls were introduced to England by way of Turkey, the English called them turkey fowls. (The much larger bird we call a turkey is, of course, not the same. The wild birds the Pilgrims discovered in the woods near

Plymouth were completely unfamiliar to them, but they did remind the English newcomers of the handsome small "turkeys" back home.)

Donkeys are smaller than horses. They have rounder bodies, thinner legs, and smaller hooves. Their coats are thicker and rougher, and their manes are shorter and their tails less hairy. Their heads seem large for their bodies, and they have Roman noses. While horses "whinny" or "neigh," donkeys "hee-haw"—their famous bray is really a piercing squeal followed by an ear-splitting roar! Donkeys are strong and surefooted, and they are generally healthy. Toughness goes together with their stubbornness, and they make better pack animals than horses. If they are trained when they are young, donkeys will work long and hard, pulling carts or carrying heavy loads on their backs.

The donkeys on these pages have a heavy gray coat with black stripes. They inherited their coloring from wild ancestors on the island of Sicily. Sicilian donkeys have a lovely pattern that extends across their backs and shoulders to form a cross. For this reason some people call them Christian donkeys or Holy Cross donkeys.

Donkeys were first kept by man about 4,000 years ago, in Egypt or Mesopotamia. (Many people believe that a donkey carried Mary and Jesus on their flight into Egypt from the Holy Land.) Donkeys are descended from the wild asses of northeast Africa. The ancestors of American donkeys came from Spain and the islands of Malta and Majorca as well as Sicily. The small burros of the American southwest and Mexico are the descendants of small asses brought along as pack animals by Spanish explorers in the 1500's.

This donkey foal, four days old, frisky and peppy, is taking off on a fast run around the pasture. She kicks up her heels just for the joy of it, scattering everything and everybody in her path. The geese flap their powerful wings and hiss their disgust, but no matter—a little donkey has to practice using her legs.

In another corner of the barnyard, fluffy chicks are strolling with their mother through the damp green grass. Here and there, down in the lower pasture, kids are scampering around in twos and threes. The lambs seem to hang back, though, a little shy. In the upper pen chunky calves with baby-bull faces try to butt the gate. The brown horse stands tall by the pasture fence while plump piglets snuffle around in the dirt at his feet.

Birds and animals, born in a barn, are growing up together on the farm. Watchful mothers coax their eager babies out to learn about the world they live in. The birds and animals of the farm share their world with all of us. We take good care of them, because they need us—and what would *we* do without *them!*

FARM ANIMALS & THEIR YOUNG

Fowl	Male	Female	Baby	Hatches in	Can survive alone
Chickens	Rooster, cock	Hen	Chick	21 days	As soon as it can eat and drink by itself. It must learn quickly because the nourishment it has had from the egg yolk lasts only a few days.
Turkeys	Tom, cock, gobbler	Hen	Poult	28 days	
Geese	Gander	Goose	Gosling	30 days	

Mammals	Male	Female	Baby	Born after	Usual litter	Must nurse
Cattle	Bull	Cow	Calf	9 months 1 week	1	5 to 8 weeks
Goats	He-goat, billy goat	She-goat, nanny goat	Kid	5 months	2, sometimes 1 or 3	2 months
Sheep	Ram	Ewe	Lamb	5 months less 5 days	1, sometimes 2	2 months
Pigs	Boar	Sow	Piglet	3 mos., 3 wks., 3 days	8 to 10	6 weeks
Horses	Stallion	Mare	Foal	11 months	1	3 months
Donkeys	Jack	Jennet, jenny	Foal	1 year (365 days)	1	3 months